THE **TESTING** SERIES

APPLICATION
FORMS

How to con

THE **TESTING** SERIES
expert advice on interview preparation

how2become

Orders: Please contact How2become Ltd, Suite 2, 50 Churchill Square Business Centre, Kings Hill, Kent ME19 4YU.

Please order via the email address info@how2become.co.uk.

ISBN: 9781907558276

First published 2011

Typeset for How2become Ltd by Molly Hill, Canada.

Printed in Great Britain for How2become Ltd by: CMP (uk) Limited, Poole, Dorset.

CONTENTS

WELCOME

Dear Sir/Madam,

Welcome to your new guide – Application Forms: How to complete them for success in your job application. This guide has been designed to teach you the art of successfully completing any job application form.

The author of this guide, Richard McMunn, has over 20 years experience in recruitment. He has successfully completed scores of job applications during his time and you will find his advice both inspiring and highly informative. As you progress through this guide you will see that there is a knack to completing job application forms correctly. Take the time to learn Richard's formula and you too can enjoy constant success when submitting any job application form, whether it is on-line or paper format.

The guide itself has been split up into useful sections to make it easier for you to prepare for each stage. Read each section carefully and take notes as you progress. The biggest piece of advice Richard will offer you is to make sure you take your time when completing any job application form. 90% of applicants will rush to complete their application form and this will be clearly evident to the person assessing the form.

If you need any further help with any selection process, then we offer a wide range of products to assist you. These are all available through our online shop www.how2become.co.uk.

Work hard, stay focused and be what you want…

Best wishes,

The how2become team

The How2become Team

PREFACE
BY RICHARD MCMUNN

Job application forms, we all detest them, right? By the time you reach the end of this guide I can assure that you will actually enjoy completing them!

The reason for this is simply because there is a knack to completing them successfully. I make no excuse, however, for stating that you must dedicate plenty of time when completing any job application form. This is where many people fall down. Having personally scored and assessed literally hundred's of forms during my time, I can spot of 'serial applicant' a mile off. A serial applicant is a person who applies for scores of jobs at any one time. Their sole purpose is to simply find paid employment. Put yourself in the shoes of the employer; would you want to employ someone who simply wanted work regardless of who it was with? No you wouldn't. You would want to employ someone who really wanted to work for your company. You would want to employ someone who was going to work hard, learn the ropes and be an enthusiastic and dedicated team player.

There are many, many tips contained within this guide that will teach you how to successfully complete a job application. Use them every time you sit down to complete an application form and you will see your success rate rapidly rise. Finally, following each sample question and response I have deliberately provided a blank template for you to create your own response. Make sure you use it and try responding to the questions. You will find that the more you practice, the better you will become.

Best wishes,

Richard McMunn

Richard McMunn

CHAPTER 1
THE PURPOSE OF AN APPLICATION FORM

Before I start to explain the most effective way to complete your job application form, it is probably best that explain the purpose of them. If you have an understanding why they are used then your chances of success will no doubt increase.

During my career I scored literally hundreds of application forms. The vast majority, I have to say, were very poor. Too many people spend too little time on their application form. Here are just a few examples of why people fail to pass the application form stage:

1. Failure to follow instructions

With your application form you should receive some form a 'guidance' notes. These will provide clear instructions on how you should complete the form. I would estimate that over 75% of people either are not aware of their existence, or they cannot be bothered to read them. For example, a form may give guidance on the colour pen that you should use. If you fail to complete the form in the designated colour, your form will most probably get rejected. If you cannot follow instructions on an application form then there is little chance that you will follow instructions in the job.

2. Poor grammar and spelling

Whatever you do, make sure you get a third party to read through your application form for errors before you submit it. In fact, if you are really serious about the job you are applying for, you may decide to pay a proof-reader to check over the form for you. An application form that is riddled with errors will be rejected.

3. Failure to meet the 'essential' criteria

Within the guidance notes or person specification for the role you are applying for, there will sometimes be a list of 'essential' and 'desirable' criteria. Make sure you match the essentials and also try to add as many desirables as possible.

4. Failure to provide suitable evidence

You will notice that, as you progress through this guide, I will encourage you to provide 'evidence' of where you meet the requirements of the job you are applying for at every opportunity. Let us assume that one of the skills required to carry out the job you are applying for is that of 'customer service'. If this is the case it is imperative that you provide some form of previous experience or qualifications in this area. This will demonstrate to the assessor that you already have some essential skills to carry out the job competently.

"The purpose of an application form is to initially assess whether or not you have the skills, qualities and attributes to perform the role. If you do, then you will be invited to attend either an assessment or an interview."

Many application forms will be 'scored' against a number of set skills, qualities and attributes and you can usually find these in the person specification or guidance notes. Take a look at the following sample person specification and in particular note the essential and desirable criteria. The position is for a customer service assistant.

SAMPLE PERSON SPECIFICATION

POST: Customer Services Assistant

ATTRIBUTES	ESSENTIAL	DESIRABLE
Qualifications/ Experience	3 GCSE/'O' levels, including Maths and English or Equivalent vocational qualification (Level 2 NVQ) or 3 years experience in customer service role and Experience of using Windows-based computer packages	Experience of working within a customer service contact centre or telephone environment Previous money handling experience
Knowledge/Skills	Ability to communicate clearly and effectively by telephone, in person and in writing Quick and accurate keyboard skills Ability to make effective decisions and work unsupervised A methodical and accurate approach to work activities Capable of following procedures and policies Excellent customer service skills Evidence of delivering a first class service to a diverse range of customers from initial point of contact	Experience of using a database including sage Handling and resolution of customer complaints from initial point of contact through to resolution

Just by reading and studying this sample person specification it is possible to predict the type of questions you could get asked both on the application form and also at the interview. Here they are:

1. Provide an example of where you have provided excellent customer service?

2. Provide an example of where you have dealt with a customer's complaint from the initial handling of the call through to resolution?

3. What knowledge or experience do you have of database systems?

4. Provide an example of when you have communicated a difficult message to a person or a group of people?

5. How do you organise your day?

6. Provide an example of where you have work effectively with a diverse range of people?

7. Provide an example of where you have solved a difficult problem whilst following procedures of policies.

Hopefully you are now starting to understand how important the person specification is when completing your application form. Whenever I have completed forms in the past I will always have at my side a copy of this important document. I will also get hold of a highlighter pen and highlight the important areas that I need to match when responding to the questions on the form. Once I match a specific requirement, I will tick it off as complete. By following this methodical approach you will be ensuring that you complete the form accurately and in line with instructions. If you do this, your chances of success will skyrocket.

GOOD RESPONSES, POOR RESPONSES AND THE STAR PRINCIPLE EXPLAINED

During this brief section of the guide I want to provide you with an example of a poor response and also a good one. I will also explain the principle that I use when responding to 'situational' application form questions. Situational questions are questions which require you to provide an example of where you have been in a specific situation, what you did whilst in that particular situation and also what the end result was.

To begin with, here's an example of a poor response to the following question:

Q1. *Provide an example of where you have worked effectively as part of a team?*

Sample response – 'poor'

"If I was to work with other people then I believe I would have the right skills to do the job correctly and professionally. I would always make sure I performed to a high standard and would work hard to get on well with other people".

The above example response is poor because it is 'generic' and it also does not answer the question. Apart from being grammatically incorrect, the person talks about what they **would** do if they worked with other people as opposed to providing evidence of where they **have** worked with other people.

Now take a look at the following 'good' response for the same question.

Sample response – 'good'

"I recently volunteered to work with a new member our team at work. The task required us both to successfully complete a stock take of the entire warehouse within a short time frame. Initially I showed the new team member how to stock take in a professional manner in accordance with company guidelines. Once I had achieved this we both then set about methodically working through each aisle, stocktaking as we went along. Periodically we would stop to ensure that the task was being done correctly. We supported each other during the task and made sure that we kept a watchful eye on the time and the progress that we were making. At the end of the specified timeframe we had completed the stock take and were able to provide accurate figures to our line manager".

The above response is effective. It conforms to the S.T.A.R principle of answering competency based questions and is also relatively easy to follow, concise and grammatically correct.

THE **S.T.A.R.** PRINCIPLE EXPLAINED

Specific – make sure your responses to each competency being assessed are specific. Provide an actual recent example of where you have met the competency. You will get marked down for being too generic. Don't say what you 'would do' but rather say what you 'have done'.

Task – briefly describe the task that you were required to carry out. In the above sample response the person has described the task in one sentence as follows:

"The task required us both to successfully complete a stock take of the entire warehouse within a short timeframe."

This sentence sets the scene and tells the person who is reading the response exactly what was required as part of your task. It is important that all of your responses follow a logical sequence of events and the STAR method allows you to do just that.

Action – during this part of your response you will detail what action you took. Remember that your response needs to be specific so you will need to state what you did, rather than what you would do in such a situation. An example of a detailed action response is as follows:

"Initially I showed the new team member how to stock take in a professional manner in accordance with company guidelines. Once I had achieved this we both then set about methodically working through each aisle, stocktaking as we went along. Periodically we would stop to ensure that the task was being done correctly."

Result – finally, at the end of your response you need to explain what the outcome was to your actions. It is always a good idea to end on a positive note. If you achieved the task successfully then you should state this. You will see from the example provided previously that the result was positive:

"At the end of the specified timeframe we had completed the stock take and were able to provide accurate figures to our line manager".

WORD COUNTS

Many employers, when requiring competency based responses to questions, will require a set 'word count' that cannot be exceeded. The reason for the word count is twofold. Firstly the employer cannot spend hours working through your responses. They receive many hundreds of applications per recruitment campaign so they need to allocate a set amount of time to each stage of the selection process. Secondly, you should be able to demonstrate your ability to meet the competencies being assessed in a few words. If you read what is required and have the ability to construct concise, yet relevant responses, then your chances of success will increase.

The maximum word count will vary from employer to employer. In my

experience I have known them to be between 100 and 500 words. If there is no allocated maximum word count, always stick to the allocated space unless directed otherwise.

The most effective way to stick within the word count is to initially create your response in Microsoft Word. By selecting 'tools' and then 'word count' you will be able to quickly assess how many words your response is. Don't go over the maximum number of words but also do not go too far under either!

CHAPTER 2
THE USE OF KEYWORDS IN YOUR RESPONSES

I strongly believe that if you use positive keywords and phrases when completing your application form your chances of success will increase. The reason for this is simple. As human beings we naturally respond in a positive manner to certain words and phrases and we also react negatively to others.

I will now list a number of keywords that you may choose to use when completing the responses to your application form. Underneath the keyword I have also provide a sample sentence of how I would personally include this in my response.

Enthusiastic

"I am a driven, hard working and enthusiastic team player."

Dedicated

"I am totally committed to my work and have a track record for being dedicated, professional and conscientious."

Committed

"I am totally committed to my work and have a track record for being dedicated, professional and conscientious."

Punctual

"I fully understand how important it is to be punctual for all work commitments and meetings."

Hardworking

"I am a driven, hard working and enthusiastic team player."

Conscientious

"My peers would describe me as someone who is highly conscientious in the workplace and who can be relied upon to deliver."

Caring

"At times I believe it is important to show compassion and, as such, I can be extremely caring when the need arises."

Teamwork

"Teamwork is the foundation of any successful business and as an employee of your company I would always do my utmost to work effectively as a team player."

Experienced

"I am highly experienced in the role that I am applying for and have numerous qualifications to my name."

Proactive

"I am a highly proactive person who is always looking for ways to improve both myself and the company that I am working for."

Focused

"I am a naturally focused person who always decides at the beginning of the day exactly what it is I aim to achieve by the end of the working day. I then go all out to achieve it."

Capable

"I have a track record for achieving and all of my appraisals state that I am a very capable person."

Meticulous

"I am a meticulous person who likes to check over my work once complete to verify its professionalism."

Organised

"I always ensure that I am organised and plan for the next working day's activities."

Persist

"If ever I am unsure how to carry out a task I will persist until I am fully competent in that particular area."

Understanding

"Having a thorough understanding of a role or a brief is crucial to its success."

Adaptable

"Although I am skilled in one particular area I am extremely adaptable and can be relied upon to assist or change roles at a moments notice."

Flexible

"I am a flexible person who can be called upon to work unsociable hours if required."

Driven

"I am a driven, hard working and enthusiastic team player."

Determined

"I am always determined to achieve any goal that is set."

Balanced

"My balanced view on things allows be to remain calm in a crisis and always perform to the best of my ability."

Achiever

"I have always been an achiever and I am not satisfied unless I have a goal to work towards at work."

Practical

"In addition to be an excellent administrative worker I am also a practical person who can adapt to any given situation."

Knowledgeable

"I always ensure that I keep myself up-to-date with work related knowledge and information that allows me to perform to the best of my abilities."

Consistent

"I am consistent in all work related activities which ensures that the work I produce is to an exceptional standard."

Analytical

"Having an analytical nature means that I am capable of helping the team solve any problems that may arise."

Compassionate

"I am always compassionate towards people whom I work with."

Independent

"Although I am an excellent team worker I am also sufficiently independent and can be relied upon to work unsupervised when required."

Cooperative

"I fully appreciate how important teamwork is in any given work related situation and I can be relied upon to be cooperative and professional at all times."

Industrious

"I have a reputation for being highly skilful and industrious."

The above list is certainly not exhaustive, however, when completing an application form I will always make good use of 'positive' keywords like these. Please feel free to use any combination of the above sentences but make sure that, if you do use them, they relate to your own skills, qualities and attributes.

It is also important to point out at this stage that you should always try wherever possible to back up your claims with 'evidence'.

Here's an example of how I would use evidence to demonstrate the quality of teamwork.

"Teamwork is the foundation of any successful business and as an employee of your company I would always do my utmost to work effectively as a team player. I already have a large amount of experience as working as part of a team. For example, in a previous role we were regularly required to work effectively as a team during stocktaking sessions. I always made sure that I communicated with each member of the team to keep them updated on my progress. I also supported the newer members of the team and provided feedback to the manager on our progress as and when required."

So, as you can see, the use of positive keywords can have a dramatic effect on your application form. They can turn it from a 'run of the mill' application form to an outstanding one.

Here's an example of how I might use positive keywords to describe my character.

"I am an experienced person who is capable of performing to a high standard in any given situation. I fully understand the importance of teamwork when in a work situation and I always ensure that I communicate effectively with other people in the team. I am cooperative, industrious and knowledgeable and I have a track record for performing well above the expected standard. Although I am a hardworking and driven person, I also know when to adapt to certain situations. For example, recently a work colleague was having a difficult time at home. I comforted her and offered to assist her in her role at work in order to take some of the pressure off her during her difficult time. I can be very compassionate and flexible when required. Finally, I believe I would make an excellent member of your team. I am enthusiastic, committed and adaptable and would perform very well in this role if the opportunity arose."

The above sample response is very positive. It is full of quality attributes that any employer would want in their team. Keep a note of the keywords that I have provided you and try to utilise them in your responses to the questions on your application form.

Now I will provide you with a number of sample application form questions and responses. Remember; take the time to create your own responses using the template provided. You can refer back to the positive keywords and phrases at anytime.

CHAPTER 3
SAMPLE QUESTIONS AND RESPONSES

This section of the guide is packed full of sample application form questions and responses. Please note: the sample responses are for guidance purposes only. They are not to be copied word for word. Instead, use them as a basis when creating your own responses.

It is also worth highlighting at this point that the majority of employers will have a copy of your application form at interview. They may ask you questions during the interview in order to verify the information you have supplied on your form. Make sure you keep a copy of your application form before you submit it and also make sure the responses you provide are true and accurate.

SAMPLE QUESTION 1

Please explain why you are applying for this post and what you have to offer.

This is a very common question. I have read many different responses to this question in the past and many of them fall at the first hurdle; they fail to respond to the questions that are being asked. If you read the question carefully you will note that there are actually two questions as follows:

Q1. Why are you applying for this post?

Q2. What do you have to offer?

I have seen people time and time again fail to answer the second part of the questions. When responding to this question split your response into two parts. The most effective way to achieve this is to start each part as follows:

Part 1

I am applying for this post because…

Part 2

I have to offer…

If you follow this piece of advice you will be ensuring that you actually answer the questions that are being asked. Always read the question very carefully before answering it.

SAMPLE RESPONSE TO QUESTION 1

Please explain why you are applying for this post and what you have to offer.

"I am applying for this post because, having studied the person specification and job description, I believe that I am very well suited to the position. I have over five years experience in a similar role, which I excelled in. I am fully aware of the requirements for this role and believe that the skills and attributes I possess would be of extreme benefit to your organisation. For example, whilst in my previous role I assisted the organisation in achieving Investors in People status. This was achieved through meticulous preparation, planning and organisation. My role was to provide the assessors with evidence of where we the organisation met each assessable criteria.

I have to offer many qualities, skills and experiences. I am a hard working, driven, ambitious and a flexible person who can be relied upon to achieve any given task. For example, in my previous role I was often asked to work late hours so that the company could meet tight deadlines. I always made sure that I was available to assist and fully realised how important these deadlines were.

To summarise, I believe that I have all of the necessary skills and qualifications to perform exceptionally in this role. I have many years experience in a similar role and can be relied upon to achieve the organisations aims and objectives."

IMPORTANT TIP: If you make reference in your application form to the company's aims and objectives, make sure you learn them before you go to interview!

Now use the template on the following page to create your own response to this question based on your own reason for applying.

Please explain why you are applying for this post and what you have to offer.

SAMPLE QUESTION 2

Please list your proficiencies, qualities, attributes and experiences that you may contribute to your performance in this post.

This type of question is asking you to 'list' proficiencies, attributes and experiences. Therefore, you may decide to answer this question with 3 lists, each headed by the specific requirement. Before you respond to this question take a look at the person specification and job description and highlight the qualities and skills required to perform the role. Then, when responding to this question, try hard to match them. In the following sample response I will use the role of a customer service assistant as an example.

SAMPLE RESPONSE TO QUESTION 2

Please list your proficiencies, qualities, attributes and experiences that you may contribute to your performance in this post.

I have a large number of exceptional qualities, attributes and proficiencies that would contribute to my performance in this post as follows:

Proficiencies

- Competent in the use of database systems both inputting and extracting data.
- Achieved NVQ in Customer service skills and the handling of complaints
- Attended and passed with distinction a 3 day Customer communication skills course

Qualities

- Ability to communicate clearly and effectively by telephone, in person and in writing
- Quick and accurate keyboard skills
- Ability to make effective decisions within established procedures
- A methodical and accurate approach to work activities
- Capable of following procedures and systematic processes
- Good organisational skills

- Capable of delivering a first class service to a diverse range of customers from initial point of contact
- Commitment to equality of opportunity and diversity
- Effective team player
- Committed to delivering first class customer service
- Able and willing to deal effectively with a diverse range of customer enquiries
- Willingness to take ownership for resolution of enquiries and complaints
- Ability to remain calm when dealing with difficult or distressed people
- Understanding of the need for confidentiality and discretion

Experiences

- 3 years experience in a customer service role
- Handling of customer complaints and enquiries
- Acted as a temporary customer service manager for 6 months to cover maternity leave

IMPORTANT TIP: Once again it is very important to obtain a copy of the person specification and job description before listing each criteria. Remember to makes sure that you include all 'ESSENTIAL' criteria and try to add as many 'DESIRABLE' as possible.

Now use the template on the following page to create your own proficiencies, qualities, attributes and experiences.

Please list your proficiencies, qualities, attributes and experiences that you may contribute to your performance in this post.

SAMPLE QUESTION 3

What evidence do you have to support your application?

As I have mentioned previously within this guide, evidence is very important. Anybody can write down on paper that they are good at a certain job, but providing actual evidence is another matter.

In the following sample response I have provided evidence of where a person meets the requirements for the role of a Sales Manager.

SAMPLE RESPONSE TO QUESTION 3

What evidence do you have to support your application?

"I am already highly experienced in the role of Sales Manager and believe that the skills, qualities and attributes I possess will be a valuable asset to your team.

To begin with I have 4 years experience at recruiting and training sales staff. In my previous role I set up a recruitment section that was responsible for headhunting the best sales staff available in the South East of England. This venture proved to be extremely successful with a retention rate of 87%. Once I had recruited the appropriate staff I then ensured they received the highest standard of training available. Each member of the team would embark on an NVQ in sales and marketing and it was my responsibility to monitor their performance in line with their appraisal.

During staff appraisals I would always monitor team morale as I believe this to be a key link to my team's high retention rate. I also have many years experience of allocating specific areas to sales executives in line with their own specific skills and qualities. Before I allocated each area I would ensure that the individual was aware of their budget and their targets for the year.

In order to keep myself abreast of company changes and policies I would keep and maintain a weekly Continuous Performance Development (CPD) folder. This essentially meant that I would allocate one hour at the beginning of every working week to CPD. The end result of this was that I was always fully up-to-date with company progress, products and services which in turn allowed me to brief my team effectively.

In terms of additional certifiable evidence I hold the following qualifications:
- BTEC National Diploma in Business (Marketing)
- Currently in the final year of my MBA

 THE **TESTING** SERIES

I also have evidence of 4 years appraisals which demonstrate that I perform to a continuously high performance."

IMPORTANT TIP: Those people who can provide firm evidence of where they meet the essential criteria have a far greater chance of being invited to assessment and interview. Remember to always focus on providing 'evidence' when completing your application form. Make it difficult for the person assessing your form to reject it!

Now use the template on the following page to create your own response to this question based on your own evidence.

What evidence do you have to support your application?

SAMPLE QUESTION 4

Describe a situation where you have worked with people who are different from you in relation to age, background or gender.

This question has been designed to assess your ability to work with others regardless of their background, age or gender. Many organisations, especially those in the Public Sector, will want to see evidence of where you have already worked with people of different ages, sex, sexual orientation, backgrounds, cultures and religious beliefs.

Remember to be specific in your response, relating it to a particular situation.

Do not be generic in your response. An example of a generic response would be – *'I am comfortable working with people from different backgrounds and have done this on many occasions'.* This type of response is not specific and does not relate to a situation. Now take a look at the following response before using a blank template to construct your own response based on your experiences.

SAMPLE RESPONSE TO QUESTION 4

Describe a situation where you have worked with people who are different from you in relation to age, background or gender.

"Whilst working in my current role as a sales assistant I was tasked with working with a new member of the team. The lady had just started working with us and was unfamiliar with the role. She was from a different background and appeared to be very nervous. I tried to comfort her and told her that I was there to support her through her first few working days and help her get her feet under the table. I fully understood how she must have felt. It was important that I supported her and helped her through her first few days at work. We are there to help each other regardless of age, background or gender. As a result of my actions the lady settled into work well and is now very happy in her role. We have been working together for 3 months and have built up a close professional and personal relationship."

IMPORTANT TIP: Try to provide an example of where you have gone out of your way to help somebody from a different background, age or gender from you. Examples that demonstrate you 'volunteered' to help, rather than having to be forced into doing it, will score higher.

Now use the template provided on the following page to create your own response to this question.

Describe a situation where you have worked with people who are different from you in relation to age, background or gender.

SAMPLE QUESTION 5

Describe a situation where you have worked closely with other people as part of a team.

In the vast number of jobs that you will apply for, having the ability to build working relationships with your colleagues is very important. Never underestimate how important teamwork is in an organisation. This question is designed to see whether you have the ability to fulfill that role. Remember again to be specific about a particular situation and avoid the pitfall of being too generic. Try to think of a situation when you have worked as part of a team, maybe to achieve a common goal or task. The following is a sample response to this question.

SAMPLE RESPONSE TO QUESTION NUMBER 5

Describe a situation where you have worked closely with other people as part of a team.

"I currently play football for a local Sunday team and we were in fear of relegation to a lower league. I offered to help the team out by arranging and coordinating an extra training session on a weekday evening so that we could look for ways to improve our skills. I felt that the team needed support and encouragement. We all needed to work together to improve our skills. I knew that unless the team pulled together and began to work closely as a unit we would be relegated. We all met up for the extra training sessions and worked on our skills and fitness whilst supporting and helping each other. I helped a team-mate to work on his fitness levels by running 3 miles with him every session. At the end of the season we managed to avoid relegation due to the combined team effort. I fully understand how important teamwork is to any organisation. I will always ensure that I work closely with other people, communicate effectively and support those people who need my assistance."

And here's another sample response to this question:

"I recently volunteered to work with a new member of our team at work. The task required us both to successfully complete a stock take of the entire warehouse within a short timeframe. The reason why I volunteered for the task is because I am a conscientious person who enjoys working with other people, and carrying out tasks to a high standard. Initially I showed the new team member how to stock take in a professional manner in accordance with company guidelines. He had never carried out this type of work before and I wanted to ensure he was both comfortable with the task and that he was doing it correctly. Once I had achieved this we both then set about methodically working through each aisle, stocktaking as we went along. Periodically we would stop to ensure that the task was being done correctly.

At the end of the specified timeframe we had completed the stock take and were able to provide accurate figures to our line manager. Whilst working as a team member I always concentrate on effective communication, focusing on the task in hand and providing support to team members who require assistance."

IMPORTANT TIP: Do not underestimate the importance of teamwork in the job that you are applying for. Most employers will want to see evidence of how you have successfully worked as part of a team in the past. The last thing they want is someone who cannot mix or work with other people. A disruptive employee/team member is every employer's worst nightmare.

Remember: the more prominent skills of a competent team member include:
- *An ability to work with anyone*
- *Always focuses on the end result or goal*
- *Able to communicate consistently and effectively*
- *Supportive of the other team members*

Once again, use the template provided on the following page to create your own unique response to this question.

Describe a situation where you have worked closely with other people as part of a team.

SAMPLE QUESTION 6

Describe a situation where you have taken steps to improve your skills and/or learn new things.

A good employee will be capable of learning new skills and improving on existing ones. Another term for this is called 'Continuous Professional Development'. Your potential employer may want to know that you have the ability to improve on your current skills and learn new things. When answering this question, try to think of an example where you have learnt something new. This may be through your working life, at home or in your leisure time. There are probably many experiences that you can draw from so take the time to think of a suitable response. I have now provided a sample response to help you.

SAMPLE RESPONSE TO QUESTION NUMBER 6

Describe a situation where you have taken steps to improve your skills and/or learn new things.

"Approximately three months ago I asked my manager at work if I could attend a two-day customer care skills course. I work as a sales assistant for a large leisure retail outlet. The course was quite in depth and whilst on it I learnt new skills including how to provide a better level of service. The reason why I took this course of action was because I wanted to improve my skills in customer care. I am always looking for ways to improve my knowledge and learn new things. I also felt that by attending the course I would be improving the level of service that our customers receive. As a result of my actions I successfully passed the course and I received a qualification in customer care skills. I feel more confident in my abilities and feel more qualified to perform my role. As a result of the course I have also improved the level of service to the customer."

IMPORTANT TIP: When you join any new job there will naturally be an element of initial training/development. It is not unreasonable, therefore, for the employer to want to see some form of evidence of where you have already taken steps to learn new skills etc. Try to provide recent examples.

Now use the template provided to create your own response.

Describe a situation where you have taken steps to improve your skills and/or learn new things.

SAMPLE QUESTION 7

Describe a situation where you have had to remain calm and controlled in a stressful situation.

Some jobs that you may apply for will require an ability to remain calm and controlled in a stressful situation. Jobs that require this type of skill include:

- High pressurised sales roles
- Dealing with members of the public
- Dealing with complaints
- Emergency services
- Call handlers and operators

When responding to this question, think of an occasion where you have had to stay calm and in control. This does not necessarily have to be in a work situation but it may be during leisure time or at home. Be careful not to answer this question generically. Focus on a particular situation that you encountered recently. Again, I have provided you with a sample response to this question.

SAMPLE RESPONSE TO QUESTION NUMBER 7

Describe a situation where you have had to remain calm and controlled in a stressful situation.

"Whilst driving home from work I came across a road accident. I parked safely and went over to see if I could help. An elderly lady was in one of the cars suffering from shock. I remained calm and dialed 999 asking for the Police and Ambulance services. Once I had done this I then gave basic First Aid to the lady and ensured that the scene was safe. The reason for taking this course of action was simply because when I arrived people were starting to panic so I knew that somebody needed to take control of the situation. By remaining calm and confident I was able to get help for the lady. As a result of my actions the emergency services soon arrived and the lady was taken to hospital. The Police then took some details of my actions and thanked me for my calm approach and for making the scene safe."

IMPORTANT TIP: Most application forms will not ask this type of question, simply because there are very few jobs that require this skill. If you are asked this question, make sure you take the time to respond to it in a comprehensive and accurate manner. Questions of this nature normally carry a lot of weight in the marking stakes!

Now use the template on the following page to create your own response to this question.

Describe a situation where you have had to remain calm and controlled in a stressful situation.

SAMPLE QUESTION 8

Describe a situation where you have had to work on your own in accordance with guidelines.

Some jobs will require an ability to work unsupervised whilst following strict guidelines and procedures. This type of question is designed to assess how trustworthy you are as a person. When answering this question, try to think of an occasion when you have worked on your own following specific guidelines. Once again, ensure that you are specific about a particular situation and avoid being too generic. The following is a sample response to this question.

SAMPLE RESPONSE TO QUESTION NUMBER 8

Describe a situation where you have had to work on your own in accordance with guidelines.

"Whilst working in my current role as a gas engineer I was tasked with fitting a new boiler to a domestic property in a safe and effective manner. I carried out this work unsupervised and was relied upon to follow strict procedural and safety guidelines. I took this course of action because if I did not follow the procedural guidance that I received during my training, then I would be putting lives at risk. I must ensure that I carry out my work responsibly and follow all safety procedures to ensure that my work is carried out in accordance with my company's policies. As a result of my actions the boiler was fitted to the required standard in accordance with the relevant British Standard and all safety procedures were followed. The customer was satisfied with my work and I was happy that I carried out my duties responsibly and in a competent manner."

Now use the template provided to create a response based on your own experiences.

Describe a situation where you have had to work on your own in accordance with guidelines.

SAMPLE QUESTION 9

*Describe a situation where you have had to change the way
you do something following a change imposed by someone
in authority.*

If an organisation or business is to improve then it must be constantly looking for ways to change, develop and modernise. In order for a company to
complete its modernisation agenda, it requires its employees to be adaptable to change. This question is designed to assess what you are like at ac-
cepting change. Some people do not like change and see it as 'change for
changes sake'. Employers want to take on people who have no issue with
change and who embrace it. When answering this question try to think of
a specific situation, either at work, home or through your leisure activities,
where a change has been imposed by someone in a position of authority.
Take a look at the following sample response to this question.

SAMPLE RESPONSE TO QUESTION NUMBER 9

*Describe a situation where you have had to change the way
you do something following a change imposed by someone
in authority.*

"Whilst working in my current job as a recruitment consultant, my manager
wanted to restructure the office and change everyone's roles and responsi-
bilities. The company was performing well but I looked upon this as an opportunity to see if we could improve even further. I fully supported my manager and offered to assist him in the process of change. I strongly believe
that change and continuous improvement is important if an organisation is
to keep on top of its game. I embrace change and look at it as a positive
thing. As a result of my supportive actions everybody soon settled into their
new roles. The change process was a success and the organisations end of
quarter figures were on the increase."

> *IMPORTANT TIP: As human beings it is only natural to be
> frightened of change. Many people in many organisations are
> reluctant to accept change. In some organisations, especially
> those that fall within the public sector, this can be a real prob-
> lem. It is important that you can embrace change as it does
> bring lots of healthy benefits.*

Use the template that follows to create your own response to this question.

Describe a situation where you have had to change the way you do something following a change imposed by someone in authority.

SAMPLE QUESTION NUMBER 10

Now that you've read more about the job, please tell us why you're applying for it and what knowledge, experience or skills you have that might be relevant.

The clue in this type of question is to READ about the job you are applying for. The question is asking you to match your knowledge, experience and skills with the job you have applied for. Therefore you need to read the job description before responding. Job descriptions or person specifications usually have both 'essential' and 'desirable' criteria included. Basically you must provide evidence of where you can meet the 'essential' criteria on your application form. Matching the desirable criteria will also gain you extra marks.

If the company you are applying for have not sent you a copy of the job description then try to obtain a copy of it before completing the form. This will give you an insight into the role that you are applying for. Once you have read the information about the post you will then be able to construct a suitable answer. Try to include any knowledge, skills or experience you may have that relates to the job description.

SAMPLE RESPONSE TO QUESTION NUMBER 10

Now that you've read more about the job, please tell us why you're applying for it and what knowledge, experience or skills you have that might be relevant.

"I am applying for this post because I am looking for a new and challenging role. I enjoy working in a customer-focused environment and believe I would make an excellent employee within your company. I understand that the company is changing and moving forward and I believe you would be an exciting company to work for. I also believe I can bring something to the team in terms of commitment, motivation and enthusiasm.

I have worked in a customer-based role for a number of years now and during this time I have developed skills that can be applied to the role that I am applying for. As well as being a good communicator and possessing excellent practical skills I am also an outstanding team player and understand that this is a very important element of the role.

I have educational qualifications in English Language, English Literature and

Art and I am also coming to the end of studying for a Diploma in Management Studies. I also hold a Health and Safety qualification through IODA in Nottingham. I am a fit and active person who visits the gym/swimming pool three times a week and I also play football for a local Sunday team. I am a very good communicator and learn new skills quickly. I am used to working long and varied hours and I understand that the role requires a high level of flexibility, which I am prepared for. I enjoy working with and meeting people from all walks of life and I truly value the benefits of a diverse workforce. To summarise, I am a highly professional, caring, trustworthy, friendly and motivated person and I believe I would make an excellent member of your organisation."

IMPORTANT TIP: Have a copy of the job description and person specification next to you when responding to this question and try to match the essential and desirable qualities.

Use the template on the following page to create your own unique response to this question.

Now that you've read more about the job, please tell us why you're applying for it and what knowledge, experience or skills you have that might be relevant.

SAMPLE QUESTION NUMBER 11

Please tell us about anything you get up to outside work that gives us a better idea of what you're like as a person and why you might be right for our company. Please give the name of the activity and what it says about you.

This type of question is designed to assess the type of person you are outside of work. This will give the company an idea of how you are likely to perform at work and will tell them if you are fit, healthy and active. When responding to this type of question, make sure you make reference to the job description. What type of duties will you be required to perform and can you match your external activities to them? Being fit and active is always a positive aspect that the assessing staff will be looking for. If you are active outside of work, then you are also likely to be active at work and achieve your tasks to the required standard. If you have recently achieved any educational or academic qualifications outside of work then it would be a good idea to make reference to these too. Now take a look at the sample response before creating your own based around your own skills, knowledge and experience.

SAMPLE RESPONSE TO QUESTION NUMBER 11

Please tell us about anything you get up to outside work that gives us a better idea of what you're like as a person and why you might be right for our company. Please give the name of the activity and what it says about you.

I attend the gym at least 3 times per week and carry out some light weight work. Whilst at the gym, I usually perform 20 minutes of rowing each time and cover a distance of 5,000 metres. I particularly enjoy swimming and swim 50 lengths, 3 times per week. When I get the opportunity I like to go walking in order to keep healthy. Staying fit and healthy means that I am able to maintain a high level of concentration at work and it also helps to keep my enthusiasm and motivation levels high. This shows that I am a dedicated and determined person who is always looking to improve himself.

I also currently play the drums and the piano. I have always enjoyed being creative and I play the drums in a function band that plays at wedding events and parties on some weekends. This shows that I have the dedication to learn new skills and I have the ability to concentrate on the task in hand when required. Learning new skills is essential to the role that I am applying for and

I believe that I have the ability to learn new skills quickly and adapt them to the work environment in a safe and effective manner.

Now use the template provided to create your own response to this question.

Please tell us about anything you get up to outside work that gives us a better idea of what you're like as a person and why you might be right for our company. Please give the name of the activity and what it says about you.

SAMPLE QUESTION NUMBER 12

Please provide examples of how you have used your initiative to solve a difficult problem.

Having the initiative to solve problems is integral to some roles, especially those that involve either a managerial or supervisory capacity. Whilst you will normally have set procedures and policies to adhere to at work you must still have the required initiative to solve difficult problems. Before responding to questions of this nature make sure you read the question very carefully first and try to understand what is required. Remember to write a response that identifies the use of your initiative to solve a difficult problem.

SAMPLE RESPONSE TO QUESTION NUMBER 12

Please provide examples of how you have used your initiative to solve a difficult problem.

"During a recent staff meeting I was aware that there were a number of problems between some members of the team. The team wasn't working effectively so we all discussed ways in which we could improve. The actions of the team were starting to have an effect on the team's performance, so I decided to take the initiative to resolve the issue. I facilitated the meeting and asked everybody to share their views and opinions. I listened to each person individually and tried to encourage people to come up with solutions in order to improve the team's effectiveness. A positive point that came from our discussions was that people felt that we didn't hold enough meetings to talk about the problems we all face. It was agreed that with immediate effect we would hold weekly meetings to discuss issues, gather and share information, and look for ways that we could all support each other in our work. Since the meeting the team has moved forward and is now working far more effectively."

Use the template on the following page to create your own response to this question.

Please provide examples of how you have used your initiative to solve a difficult problem.

SAMPLE QUESTION NUMBER 13

Please provide a recent example of how you have developed your abilities to improve yourself.

Having the ability to constantly review your own performance and take steps to improve is an important aspect of everyday life. This is particularly relevant in the workplace and the majority of employers would rather take on someone who is capable of improving and developing.

When responding to this type of question try to think of an example or examples where you have improved yourself. This may be through a training course or educational qualification(s). This type of question is sometimes asked on application forms where the post applied for involves some form of intensive initial training course.

SAMPLE RESPONSE TO QUESTION NUMBER 13

Please provide a recent example of how you have developed your abilities to improve yourself.

"In order to carry out my duties in my current role effectively I felt that I needed more management skills. I decided to pay for, and embark on, a Diploma Course in Management. I am coming to the end of the course and have found it a useful tool for improving my skills. I am always looking for new ways to improve my skills and knowledge so that I can perform better both in a professional and personal capacity. I also believe it is important to keep fully up-to-date and conversant with company policies. Every week I read the company policy update log to ensure I am fully aware of any changes or amendments to working practices."

Use the template that follows to create your response to this question.

Please provide a recent example of how you have developed your abilities to improve yourself.

SAMPLE QUESTION NUMBER 14

Please provide an example of how you have played a positive role as team member or leader.

This type of question may be asked on application forms for jobs that involve a managerial or supervisory role. Try to think of an occasion when you have been part of a team or have even been the leader of a team. When responding to questions of this nature think of a scenario where you worked as part of the team to achieve a task or solve a problem. Now take a look at the following sample response before using the template to construct your own.

SAMPLE RESPONSE TO QUESTION NUMBER 14

Please provide an example of how you have played a positive role as team member or leader.

"In my current role I am responsible for the safety of my team and for ensuring that any health and safety incidents are reported in line with company regulations. I am also involved in coaching and mentoring my team and providing them with feedback, often helping them to improve. I currently lead a team of 18 staff and I am required to ensure the team operates effectively in terms of management, health and safety, and training. Following any incident that relates to health and safety I always fully brief each member of the team to ensure that I have done everything in my power to prevent an incident occurring again. In particular I recently carried out the appraisals of all of my staff. This was a long and difficult process but it was important that I was thorough and consistent in my approach. I identified that two members of the team required development in specific areas so I arranged for consolidation training to be undertaken. This action resulted in improved performance for both of them. As a leader it is my responsibility to identify problems within my team and act accordingly."

Now use the template that follows to create your own response to this question.

Please provide an example of how you have played a positive role as team member or leader.

SAMPLE QUESTION NUMBER 15

Please provide an example of how you have had to work under pressure.

Some careers will require you to work under pressure or to tight deadlines. Examples of this type of role include:

• Sales manager/executive

• Managerial/Executive positions

• Traders

• Train Drivers

• Emergency Service workers

• Emergency Service Call Handlers

When responding to this question try to think of a scenario where you have worked under pressure but still achieved the task or goal.

Take a look at the following sample response before using the template to construct your own.

SAMPLE RESPONSE TO QUESTION NUMBER 15

Please provide an example of how you have had to work under pressure.

"In my current role as customer service manager I am required to work under pressure on a daily basis. Recently, I was presented with a situation where two members of staff had gone sick leaving me with only three other staff members to manage the shop during a busy Saturday.

During the morning we were due to take a stock delivery which meant that I had to perform many tasks without taking a break. During the day I dealt with two customer complaints, took delivery of the stock, served customers whilst others took their break and also dealt with a fire alarm actuation. In order to achieve each task I both prioritised my workload and delegated roles that could be carried out by someone else to another employee. I maintained a calm and composed attitude throughout the day and always focused on the task in hand. I am often required to perform under pressure and thrive in such conditions. I always adapt well to situations like these and ensure that I still maintain a high level of professionalism at all times."

Now use the template on the following page to create your own unique response to this question.

Please provide an example of how you have had to work under pressure.

SAMPLE QUESTION NUMBER 16

Please provide an example of how you have taken responsibility to communicate an important message.

Some roles will require you to communicate messages to groups of people. Sometimes that message might be bad news or have a negative impact on someone's day. Try to think of an occasion where you have had to communicate an important message where you were under pressure. Take a look at the following sample response which will help you to create your own. Once you have read the provided example, use the template provided to construct your own response based on your own experiences.

SAMPLE RESPONSE TO QUESTION NUMBER 16

Please provide an example of how you have taken responsibility to communicate an important message.

"Whilst working in my current position as a sales person I was the duty manager for the day as my manager had gone sick. It was the week before Christmas and the shop was very busy. During the day the fire alarm went off and I started to ask everybody to evacuate the shop, which is our company policy. The alarm has gone off in the past but the normal manager usually lets people stay in the shop whilst he finds out if it's a false alarm. This was a difficult situation because the shop was very busy, nobody wanted to leave, and my shop assistants were disagreeing with me in my decision to evacuate the shop. Some of the customers were becoming irate as they were in the changing rooms at the time. Both the customers and my shop assistants were disagreeing with me. The customers were saying that it was appalling that they had to evacuate the shop and that they would complain to the head office about it. My sales staff were trying to persuade me to keep everybody inside the shop and that it was most probably a false alarm, like it usually is. I was determined to evacuate everybody from the shop for safety reasons and would not allow anybody to deter me from my aim. The safety of my staff and customers was at the forefront of my mind, even though it wasn't at theirs. I persisted with my actions and eventually got everybody to leave the shop. When the Fire Service arrived they informed me that there had been a small fire at the rear of the shop and that the actions I had taken were the right ones. Everybody was safe and nobody was hurt as a result of the incident."

And here's another example of where somebody had to deliver a difficult message:

"Whilst working as a mechanic in my current job I was faced with a situation where a customer, following a routine service, did not want to have an important piece of safety critical work carried out on her car. My task was to explain to her the dangers that she faced by not having the work carried out, and influence her to proceed with the work. I started out by explaining in simple terms the reason for the fault and the fact that she had been driving around with this dangerous problem for some time. I also explained the consequences of not having the work carried out as a matter of urgency and reassured her that the problem was genuine. After careful communication and a detailed explanation of the problem and the dangers she faced, she finally agreed to have the work carried out there and then. I fully understood how she must have been feeling and was sensitive in my communication approach. The result was that the lady would now have a safe car to drive and therefore herself and her family would not be exposed to any unnecessary dangers."

Now use the template on the following page to create your own response to this question.

Please provide an example of how you have taken responsibility to communicate an important message.

QUESTION NUMBER 17

Give an example of where you have dealt effectively with a customer complaint

People who work in sales generally have to deal with customer complaints. Therefore, if you are applying for a job of this nature you may have to respond to this type of question on your application form. Make sure you provide an example of where you went out of your way to resolve the issue. Take a look at the following sample response.

SAMPLE RESPONSE TO QUESTION NUMBER 17

Give an example of where you have dealt effectively with a customer complaint

"Whilst working as a sales representative for my current employer, I received a telephone call from an unhappy customer. It was my task to resolve the situation to his satisfaction whilst operating in accordance with company guidelines. I started out by listening very carefully and attentively to his concerns and taking detailed notes about his complaint. I informed him that I fully understood his concerns and I reassured him that I would do everything possible to help him and to resolve the issue. The complaint centered on an order which he had placed online. His parcel had not yet arrived and it was now 2 weeks since the order was placed. I immediately dispatched another order priority delivery whilst on the phone to him, making sure that the order would be delivered that same day. I also informed him that I would call him later that day to make sure he was happy with the new order. To make sure that he was fully satisfied with my actions I provided him with a unique tracking number for his new order. Later that day, I telephoned the gentleman to check that everything was to his satisfaction. The sound in his voice was very rewarding and I realised that with just a little help I had made such a difference to his day, making him feel like a valued customer. The result of the situation was that an initially unhappy customer was now happy with the service he had received and the company had maintained its positive image."

Now use the template that follows to create your own response.

Give an example of where you have dealt effectively with a customer complaint

CHAPTER 4
FINAL TIPS FOR COMPLETING A SUCCESSFUL APPLICATION

In this final section of the guide I will provide you with a number of useful tips that will help you when completing your application form.

> It is very important that you read the entire application form first before attempting to complete it. It is also important that you obtain a copy of the guidance notes that accompany the form. These notes will normally provide you with some important tips on how you are expected to complete the form.

> Have at your side a copy of the person specification and job description when completing the form. Try as hard as possible to match the assessable qualities.

> Make sure you match the 'essential' criteria when completing the form. This is how you will be assessed. If you do not meet all of the essential criteria then you may not get invited to the next stage.

> Before I complete an application form I will read through the person specification, job description and guidance notes and use a highlighter pen to highlight the important areas and skills that I need to match. This way I am guaranteed to complete the form in accordance with the employer's requirements.

> Make sure you follow ALL instructions. If the form asks for 'black ink' and 'block capitals', make sure you use them!

> Many forms get rejected through improper spelling and poor grammar. If you are weak in these areas you should get someone who is competent to check for errors. If you are really serious about completing a great application form you may decide to get your responses proofread.

> If there is a word count on the form do not go over it. A great way to check your word count is to carry out an initial draft of your response using Microsoft Word. If you click Tools/Word count, this will tell you the exact word count which will save you having to count each individual word!

> When responding to competency based questions you need to provide specific examples of when you used the assessable skills.

> Always try to provide 'evidence' of where you match the qualities being assessed.

> Use the STAR method when responding to situational questions. Another example of how to structure your responses is as follows:

CARA

Context– set the scene

Action – what you did or the skills used

Result – the outcome

After – what you learned from the experience

Make sure you focus on what you specifically did and not on what others did.

> Before you submit your form make sure you keep a copy of it for reference. You may need it at the interview.

Visit www.how2become.co.uk to find more titles and courses that will help you to pass any job or career selection process, including:

- Interview Skills Books

- 1 Day intensive training courses

- Online interview training and psychometric testing

- Psychometric testing books and CD's

www.how2become.co.uk